MY
WELL-BEING
journal

My Well Being Journal

© Sharon Witt
September 2020

Published by Collective Wisdom Publications Pty Ltd
PO Box 150
Mt Evelyn Victoria 3796

www.sharonwitt.com.au

A catalogue record for this
work is available from the
National Library of Australia

Design: Ivan Smith, Communiqué Graphics, Lilydale
Printed in Australia by Openbook Howden Print & Design

NAME

··

'You may not control all the events that happen to you, but you can decide not to be reduced by them.'

Maya Angelou

Dear amazing, strong, resilient lady,

I am so pleased that you are holding your own journal in your hands right now.

What I want to say to you right now, is this….

You are not alone!

THIS JOURNAL has been created especially for you!

A place to record your thoughts, emotions, ideas, frustrations and day to day responses.

I'm using it right alongside you.

I have set out this journal so that you can record your emotions and ideas each day. I've also included some helpful quotes, and space to set some goals. You do not have to use it every single day, but I find when you choose to make something a regular thing, it forms a habit. I've also included space to encourage you to connect with at least one other person each day, and think about some dreams for the future.

I've also included some ideas for self-care – this is important!

Just as the pilot instructs us during the safety demonstration on flights – we must give ourselves oxygen first, before we can then give it to others.

Best wishes and take care,

Sharon

Using your journal

You will notice that there is a double page set aside for each day. You may choose to make it a HABIT and write in your journal each day. Or you may choose to fill pages in on the days you feel like you want to check in.

If you write in your journal each day, you will soon notice that not every day is the SAME. If you are anything like me, I find I might experience a few really great days – when I feel like I can get so much done and I'm firing on all cylinders. And then, I can feel just 'blergh' with very little energy or motivation. This is perfectly normal.

 Checking In

Each page has a few different pictures of emotions. Circle the one that best describes you right now. How are you feeling today?

Is there any particular reason or event that has brought this feeling today?

Sometimes, we can feel frustrated, stressed, happy, worried, anxious, excited – a whole range of emotions. Sometimes, we might just feel a bit *blerghhh* and not sure why. It may just help to RECOGNISE the feelings and emotions you are feeling on a particular day.

You may want to write why you might be feeling that way, or maybe you don't even know why. That's okay ☺.

Three goals for today

As a teacher, I often have TOO MANY things that I have to do each day and I can feel very overwhelmed. So do you know what I do? I write a list of THREE things I need to do that day – just three. That way, I can tick them off or cross them out when I've completed them. You may only get one completed. That's ok. Be kind to yourself. Set it for another day again if it's important.

Space to write or draw

Sometimes, we just need space to write, scribble, or just draw random things.

Three things I am thankful for today

We can always find something to be grateful for each day. When we practice gratitude we build resilience. It is a helpful habit to get into the habit of finding 3 things you can be thankful for each day. No matter what has happened in your day, you can always find things that are going well for you (some days we might just have to look a bit harder ☺). You might be thankful for a warm bed, a cuddle with your pet, watching a movie, a nice meal you ate, a chance to connect with a friend or just that the internet was working properly today!

One thing I did for someone else today

When we are facing challenging times, I always find it helpful to take my mind off how I may be feeling by doing something for someone else. And it always makes me feel better.

Ideas might include: writing a letter to a friend or relative and posting it, calling, texting or facetiming a friend, making a homemade gift for someone, or sending flowers, wine or chocolate to someone.

One thing that went well for me today

I don't know about you- but some days are tough and it just seems like I'm not getting anywhere! So I look for one thing that DID go well that day. Focus on the positive ☺.

One dream I have for the future

Use this space each day to dream of something you want to do – both small dreams and BIG dreams.

One person I will connect with today

It's important to maintain connection with others, including friends and family. You may also choose to connect in with other helpful professionals. This space in your journal each day, reminds you that it's important to connect.

One thing I can do for self-care today

This can be as little as making yourself a cup of tea and sitting outside for ten minutes, to running a bath, lighting candles and soaking in the quiet for an hour. I have included a full list of some selfcare ideas in this journal.

One thing I can do for my body today

Aim to do something each day to nourish or move your body. This might be going for a 20-minute walk, doing some exercise, making a really healthy breakfast or lunch, or even just taking some time to rest your mind such as laying outside and listening to some music (your brain is an important part of your body.)

'Our greatest weakness lies in giving up. The most certain way to succeed is always to try just one more time.'

Thomas Edison

Check in

Today's date:

How am I feeling today?

... and why?

Three goals I have for today:

1.

2.

3.

Free space to write or draw

Write three things that you are thankful for today:

Thankful

One thing I can do for self-care today:

One dream I have for the future:

One thing I can do to care for my body today:

One person I can connect with today:

What went well for me today:

'Success is liking yourself, liking what you do and liking how you do it.'

Maya Angelou

Check in

Today's date:

How am I feeling today?

... and why?

Three goals I have for today:

1.

2.

3.

Free space to write or draw

Write three things that you are thankful for today:

One thing I can do for self-care today:

One dream I have for the future:

One thing I can do to care for my body today:

One person I can connect with today:

What went well for me today:

'Education is the most powerful weapon which you can use to change the world.'

Nelson Mandela

Check in

Today's date:

_____

How am I feeling today?

_____

... and why?

_____

_____

_____

_____

Three goals I have for today:

1.

_____

_____

2.

_____

_____

3.

_____

_____

Free space to write or draw

Write three things that you are thankful for today:

One thing I can do for
self-care today:

One dream I have for the
future:

One thing I can do to care
for my body today:

One person I can connect with today:

What went well for me today:

'Yesterday is gone.
Tomorrow has not yet come.
We have only today. Let us begin.'
Mother Teresa

 **Check in**

Today's date:

How am I feeling today?

....

... and why?

....

....

....

....

Three goals I have for today:

1.

....

2.

....

3.

....

Free space to write or draw

Write three things that you are thankful for today:

Thankful

One thing I can do for self-care today:

One dream I have for the future:

One thing I can do to care for my body today:

One person I can connect with today:

What went well for me today:

'Reading is important.
If you know how to read,
the whole world opens up to you.'

Barack Obama

Check in

Today's date:

How am I feeling today?

... and why?

Three goals I have for today:

1.

2.

3.

Free space to write or draw

Write three things that you are thankful for today:

One thing I can do for self-care today:

One dream I have for the future:

One thing I can do to care for my body today:

One person I can connect with today:

What went well for me today:

'You get in life what you have the courage to ask for.'

Oprah Winfrey

SELF-CARE SUGGESTIONS

- Make your favourite cup of tea and read a book.

- Go for a 20-minute walk.

- Look up a recipe and bake something yummy.

- Write a letter or card to a friend you haven't connected with in a while. Send it by snail mail for a change.

- Run yourself a bubble bath, light a candle and relax and read for 30 minutes.

- Wash and blow dry your hair.

- Paint your nails.

- Take yourself on a date to the movies.

'Real generosity is
doing something
nice for someone
who will never
find out.'
Frank A. Clark

Check in

How am I feeling today?

... and why?

Three goals I have for today:

1.

2.

3.

Free space to write or draw

Write three things that you are thankful for today:

Thankful

One thing I can do for self-care today:

One dream I have for the future:

One thing I can do to care for my body today:

One person I can connect with today:

What went well for me today:

_'Don't count the days.
Make the days count.'_

Muhammad Ali

Check in

How am I feeling today?

... and why?

Three goals I have for today:

1.

2.

3.

Free space to write or draw

Write three things that you are thankful for today:

One thing I can do for self-care today:

One dream I have for the future:

One thing I can do to care for my body today:

One person I can connect with today:

What went well for me today:

'You must be the change you wish to see in the world.'

Mahatma Ghandi

Check in

Today's date:

How am I feeling today?

... and why?

Three goals I have for today:

1.

2.

3.

Free space to write or draw

Write three things that you are thankful for today:

One thing I can do for self-care today:

One dream I have for the future:

One thing I can do to care for my body today:

One person I can connect with today:

What went well for me today:

'My mission in life is not merely to survive but to thrive.'

Maya Angelou

 # Check in

Today's date:

_____

How am I feeling today?

_____

_____

... and why?

_____

_____

_____

_____

_____

Three goals I have for today:

1. _____

_____

2. _____

_____

3. _____

Free space to write or draw

Write three things that you are thankful for today:

Thankful

One thing I can do for self-care today:

One dream I have for the future:

One thing I can do to care for my body today:

One person I can connect with today:

What went well for me today:

'If I cannot do great things, I can do small things in a great way.'

Martin Luther King Jr.

Check in

Today's date:

How am I feeling today?

... and why?

Three goals I have for today:

1.

2.

3.

Free space to write or draw

Write three things that you are thankful for today:

One thing I can do for self-care today:

One dream I have for the future:

One thing I can do to care for my body today:

One person I can connect with today:

What went well for me today:

*'You are enough,
just as you are.'*
Meghan Markle

Check in

How am I feeling today?

... and why?

Three goals I have for today:

1.

2.

3.

Free space to write or draw

Write three things that you are thankful for today:

One thing I can do for self-care today:

One dream I have for the future:

One thing I can do to care for my body today:

One person I can connect with today:

What went well for me today:

'I can't change the direction of the wind, but I can adjust my sails to always reach my destination.'

Jimmy Dean

Check in

Today's date:

How am I feeling today?

... and why?

Three goals I have for today:

1.

2.

3.

Free space to write or draw

Write three things that you are thankful for today:

Thankful

One thing I can do for self-care today:

One dream I have for the future:

One thing I can do to care for my body today:

One person I can connect with today:

What went well for me today:

'Don't be afraid. Be focussed. Be determined.
Be hopeful. Be powerful.'

Barack Obama

Check in

Today's date:

How am I feeling today?

... and why?

Three goals I have for today:

1.

2.

3.

Free space to write or draw

Write three things that you are thankful for today:

One thing I can do for self-care today:

One dream I have for the future:

One thing I can do to care for my body today:

One person I can connect with today:

What went well for me today:

'Know what sparks the light in you so that you, in your own way, can illuminate the world.'

Oprah Winfrey

 Check in

Today's date:

How am I feeling today?

... and why?

Three goals I have for today:

1.

2.

3.

Free space to write or draw

Write three things that you are thankful for today:

Thankful

One thing I can do for self-care today:

One dream I have for the future:

One thing I can do to care for my body today:

One person I can connect with today:

What went well for me today:

'Be yourself;
everyone else is already taken.'

Oscar Wilde

Check in

Today's date:

How am I feeling today?

... and why?

Three goals I have for today:

1.

2.

3.

Free space to write or draw

Write three things that you are thankful for today:

One thing I can do for self-care today:

One dream I have for the future:

One thing I can do to care for my body today:

One person I can connect with today:

What went well for me today:

'Live as if you were to die tomorrow.
Learn as if you were to live forever.'

Mahatma Gandhi

'Once she stopped rushing through life, she was amazed at how much more life she had time for.'

SELF-CARE SUGGESTIONS

- Take yourself out for lunch.

- Create a gratitude book/jar and take 5 minutes each day to write one thing for which you are grateful.

- Begin taking a photo each day to record something for which you are grateful.
  You can have this made into a photo book once the 12 months is up.

- Meet a friend in a café for lunch or coffee.

- Paint.

- Draw.

- Colour in.

- Write.

 Check in

Today's date:

How am I feeling today?

... and why?

Three goals I have for today:

1.

2.

3.

Free space to write or draw

Write three things that you are thankful for today:

Thankful

One thing I can do for self-care today:

One dream I have for the future:

One thing I can do to care for my body today:

One person I can connect with today:

What went well for me today:

'I really think a champion is defined not by their wins but by how they can recover when they fall.'

Serena Williams

Check in

Today's date:

How am I feeling today?

... and why?

Three goals I have for today:

1.

2.

3.

Free space to write or draw

Write three things that you are thankful for today:

Thankful

One thing I can do for self-care today:

One dream I have for the future:

One thing I can do to care for my body today:

One person I can connect with today:

What went well for me today:

'At the end of the day, we can endure much more than we think we can.'

Frida Kahlo

Check in

Today's date:

_____

How am I feeling today?

_____

_____

... and why?

_____

_____

_____

_____

_____

Three goals I have for today:

1.

_____

_____

2.

_____

_____

3.

_____

_____

Free space to write or draw

Write three things that you are thankful for today:

One thing I can do for self-care today:

One dream I have for the future:

One thing I can do to care for my body today:

One person I can connect with today:

What went well for me today:

'Just one small, positive thought in the morning can change your whole day.'

Dalai Lama

Check in

Today's date:

How am I feeling today?

... and why?

Three goals I have for today:

1.

2.

3.

Free space to write or draw

Write three things that you are thankful for today:

Thankful

One thing I can do for self-care today:

One dream I have for the future:

One thing I can do to care for my body today:

One person I can connect with today:

What went well for me today:

*'Let us remember:
One book, one pen, one child and one teacher can change the world.'*

Malala Yousafzai

Check in

Today's date:

How am I feeling today?

... and why?

Three goals I have for today:

1.

2.

3.

Free space to write or draw

Write three things that you are thankful for today:

One thing I can do for self-care today:

One dream I have for the future:

One thing I can do to care for my body today:

One person I can connect with today:

What went well for me today:

*'You cannot shake hands
with a clenched fist.'*

Indira Gandhi

 **Check in**

Today's date:

How am I feeling today?

... and why?

Three goals I have for today:

1.

2.

3.

Free space to write or draw

Write three things that you are thankful for today:

Thankful

One thing I can do for self-care today:

One dream I have for the future:

One thing I can do to care for my body today:

One person I can connect with today:

What went well for me today:

_'The cure for boredom is curiosity.
There is no cure for curiosity.'_

Dorothy Parker

 Check in

Today's date:

How am I feeling today?

... and why?

Three goals I have for today:

1.

2.

3.

Free space to write or draw

Write three things that you are thankful for today:

Thankful

One thing I can do for self-care today:

One dream I have for the future:

One thing I can do to care for my body today:

One person I can connect with today:

What went well for me today:

*'Let us pick up our books and our pencils,
they are our most powerful weapons.'*

Malala Yousafzai

Check in

How am I feeling today?

... and why?

Three goals I have for today:

1.

2.

3.

Free space to write or draw

Write three things that you are thankful for today:

One thing I can do for self-care today:

One dream I have for the future:

One thing I can do to care for my body today:

One person I can connect with today:

What went well for me today:

*'I alone cannot change the world,
but I can cast a stone across the water to
create many ripples.'*

Mother Teresa

Check in

How am I feeling today?

... and why?

Three goals I have for today:

1.

2.

3.

Free space to write or draw

Write three things that you are thankful for today:

One thing I can do for self-care today:

One dream I have for the future:

One thing I can do to care for my body today:

One person I can connect with today:

What went well for me today:

'The true delight is in the finding out rather than in the knowing.'

Isaac Asimov

 Check in

Today's date:

How am I feeling today?

... and why?

Three goals I have for today:

1.

2.

3.

Free space to write or draw

Write three things that you are thankful for today:

Thankful

One thing I can do for self-care today:

One dream I have for the future:

One thing I can do to care for my body today:

One person I can connect with today:

What went well for me today:

'Keep your face always towards the sunshine and the shadows will fall behind you.'

Walt Whitman

SELF-CARE SUGGESTIONS

- Lay on your bed or couch and listen to some relaxing music (just go on You Tube and search relaxation music).

- Watch your favourite chick-flick or comedy movie.

- Make a Pinterest Board (actually, on second thoughts – you may poke your head up and realise you've just time-lapsed 8 hours!! ☺)

- Create a dream board.

- Lay on the grass outside and daydream.

- Start a hobby such as jewellery making, hand-made crafts, photography.

- Crochet or knit
  (And NO! This is NOT JUST for the older, retired woman! Some of my dearest YOUNG female friends are crocheting and knitting up a storm to relax!!)

'It is never too late to be what you might have been.'

George Eliot

Check in

How am I feeling today?

... and why?

Three goals I have for today:

1.

2.

3.

Free space to write or draw

Write three things that you are thankful for today:

One thing I can do for self-care today:

One dream I have for the future:

One thing I can do to care for my body today:

One person I can connect with today:

What went well for me today:

'When people are determined, they can overcome anything.'

Nelson Mandela

 **Check in**

Today's date:

How am I feeling today?

... and why?

Three goals I have for today:

1.

2.

3.

Free space to write or draw

Write three things that you are thankful for today:

Thankful

One thing I can do for self-care today:

One dream I have for the future:

One thing I can do to care for my body today:

One person I can connect with today:

What went well for me today:

'You may not control all the events that happen to you, but you can decide not to be reduced by them.'

Maya Angelou

Check in

Today's date:

How am I feeling today?

... and why?

Three goals I have for today:

1.

2.

3.

Free space to write or draw

Write three things that you are thankful for today:

One thing I can do for self-care today:

One dream I have for the future:

One thing I can do to care for my body today:

One person I can connect with today:

What went well for me today:

'The best way to not feel hopeless
is to get up and do something.'

Barack Obama

 **Check in**

Today's date:

How am I feeling today?

... and why?

Three goals I have for today:

1.

2.

3.

Free space to write or draw

Write three things that you are thankful for today:

Thankful

One thing I can do for self-care today:

One dream I have for the future:

One thing I can do to care for my body today:

One person I can connect with today:

What went well for me today:

'Alone time is when I distance myself from the voices of the world so I can hear my own.'

Oprah Winfrey

Check in

How am I feeling today?

... and why?

Three goals I have for today:

1.

2.

3.

Free space to write or draw

Write three things that you are thankful for today:

One thing I can do for
self-care today:

One dream I have for the
future:

One thing I can do to care
for my body today:

One person I can connect with today:

What went well for me today:

*'Let us make our future now, and let us
make our dreams tomorrow's reality.'*

Malala Yousafzai

Check in

How am I feeling today?

_____

... and why?

_____
_____
_____
_____
_____

Three goals I have for today:

1. _____
_____

2. _____
_____

3. _____
_____

Free space to write or draw

Write three things that you are thankful for today:

One thing I can do for self-care today:

One dream I have for the future:

One thing I can do to care for my body today:

One person I can connect with today:

What went well for me today:

'Your playing small does not serve the world. Who are you not to be great?'

Nelson Mandela

Check in

Today's date:

How am I feeling today?

... and why?

Three goals I have for today:

1.

2.

3.

Free space to write or draw

Write three things that you are thankful for today:

Thankful

One thing I can do for self-care today:

One dream I have for the future:

One thing I can do to care for my body today:

One person I can connect with today:

What went well for me today:

'If my mind can conceive it and my heart can believe it, then I can achieve it.'

Muhammad Ali

Check in

How am I feeling today?

...and why?

Three goals I have for today:

1.

2.

3.

Free space to write or draw

Write three things that you are thankful for today:

One thing I can do for self-care today:

One dream I have for the future:

One thing I can do to care for my body today:

One person I can connect with today:

What went well for me today:

'You can't use up creativity. The more you use, the more you have.'

Maya Angelou

 Check in

Today's date:

_____

How am I feeling today?

_____
_____

... and why?

_____
_____
_____
_____
_____

Three goals I have for today:

1. _____

_____

2. _____

_____

3. _____

Free space to write or draw

Write three things that you are thankful for today:

Thankful

One thing I can do for self-care today:

One dream I have for the future:

One thing I can do to care for my body today:

One person I can connect with today:

What went well for me today:

'No matter what happens, the sun will rise in the morning.'

Barack Obama

Check in

Today's date:

How am I feeling today?

... and why?

Three goals I have for today:

1.

2.

3.

Free space to write or draw

Write three things that you are thankful for today:

One thing I can do for
self-care today:

One dream I have for the
future:

One thing I can do to care
for my body today:

One person I can connect with today:

What went well for me today:

*'We must use time creatively,
and forever realise that the time
is always ripe to do right.'*

Nelson Mandela

Believe you
can and
you're
halfway
there
Theodore
Roosevelt

SELF-CARE SUGGESTIONS

- Sing, play an instrument (or learn to play).

- Write song lyrics.

- Moisturise your skin.

- Take photos of nature or items that inspire you.

- Hop into bed under the doona and binge-watch your favourite TV series.

- Go for a bike ride.

- Sew – create things out of recycled garments from the local op shop.

- Set up a tent in your backyard for a night and go 'glamping' on your own.

Check in

Today's date:

How am I feeling today?

... and why?

Three goals I have for today:

1.

2.

3.

Free space to write or draw

Write three things that you are thankful for today:

Thankful

One thing I can do for self-care today:

One dream I have for the future:

One thing I can do to care for my body today:

One person I can connect with today:

What went well for me today:

'This moment is as true as testament there is to the human spirit.'

Prince Harry and Meghan Markle

Check in

Today's date:

How am I feeling today?

😄 😊 😌 😐 😟 😣

_____

... and why?

_____
_____
_____
_____
_____

Three goals I have for today:

1.
_____
_____

2.
_____
_____

3.
_____
_____

Free space to write or draw

Write three things that you are thankful for today:

_____   _____   _____

_____   _____   _____

_____   _____   _____

_____   _____   _____

_____   _____   _____

One thing I can do for self-care today:

_____

_____

_____

_____

One dream I have for the future:

_____

_____

_____

_____

One thing I can do to care for my body today:

_____

_____

_____

_____

One person I can connect with today:

_____

_____

_____

_____

_____

What went well for me today:

_____

_____

_____

'May your choices reflect your hopes, not your fears.'

Nelson Mandela

Check in

Today's date:

How am I feeling today?

...and why?

Three goals I have for today:

1.

2.

3.

Free space to write or draw

Write three things that you are thankful for today:

_____   _____   _____

_____   _____   _____

_____   _____   _____

_____   _____   _____

One thing I can do for self-care today:

_____

_____

_____

_____

One dream I have for the future:

_____

_____

_____

_____

One thing I can do to care for my body today:

_____

_____

_____

_____

One person I can connect with today:

_____

_____

_____

_____

What went well for me today:

_____

_____

_____

_____

'Do the best you can until you know better.
Then when you know better, do better.'

Maya Angelou

 **Check in**

Today's date:

How am I feeling today?

... and why?

Three goals I have for today:

1.

2.

3.

Free space to write or draw

Write three things that you are thankful for today:

Thankful

One thing I can do for self-care today:

One dream I have for the future:

One thing I can do to care for my body today:

One person I can connect with today:

What went well for me today:

'I am grateful for my victories, but I am especially grateful for my losses, because they only made me work harder.'
Muhammad Ali

Check in

How am I feeling today?

😄 😊 😌 😐 ☹️ 😣

... and why?

Three goals I have for today:

1.

2.

3.

Free space to write or draw

Write three things that you are thankful for today:

_____ _____ _____

_____ _____ _____

_____ _____ _____

_____ _____ _____

_____ _____ _____

One thing I can do for self-care today:

_____

_____

_____

_____

One dream I have for the future:

_____

_____

_____

_____

One thing I can do to care for my body today:

_____

_____

_____

_____

One person I can connect with today:

_____

_____

_____

_____

What went well for me today:

_____

_____

_____

'It always seems impossible until it is done.'

Nelson Mandela

 Check in

Today's date:

How am I feeling today?

... and why?

Three goals I have for today:

1.

2.

3.

Free space to write or draw

Write three things that you are thankful for today:

Thankful

One thing I can do for self-care today:

One dream I have for the future:

One thing I can do to care for my body today:

One person I can connect with today:

What went well for me today:

'If your dreams don't scare you, they aren't big enough.'

Muhammad Ali

Check in

How am I feeling today?

... and why?

Three goals I have for today:

1.

2.

3.

Free space to write or draw

Write three things that you are thankful for today:

Thankful

One thing I can do for self-care today:

One dream I have for the future:

One thing I can do to care for my body today:

One person I can connect with today:

What went well for me today:

'Shoot for the moon. Even if you miss, you'll land among stars!'

Les Brown

Check in

Today's date:

How am I feeling today?

... and why?

Three goals I have for today:

1.

2.

3.

Free space to write or draw

Write three things that you are thankful for today:

One thing I can do for self-care today:

One dream I have for the future:

One thing I can do to care for my body today:

One person I can connect with today:

What went well for me today:

'Believe you can and you're halfway there.'

Theodore Roosevelt

Check in

How am I feeling today?

... and why?

Three goals I have for today:

1.

2.

3.

Free space to write or draw

Write three things that you are thankful for today:

Thankful

One thing I can do for self-care today:

One dream I have for the future:

One thing I can do to care for my body today:

One person I can connect with today:

What went well for me today:

'It's not that I'm so smart, it's just that I stay with problems longer.'

Albert Einstein

Check in

Today's date:

How am I feeling today?

... and why?

Three goals I have for today:

1.

2.

3.

Free space to write or draw

Write three things that you are thankful for today:

One thing I can do for self-care today:

One dream I have for the future:

One thing I can do to care for my body today:

One person I can connect with today:

What went well for me today:

'It always seems impossible until it is done.'

Nelson Mandela

 **Check in**

Today's date:

How am I feeling today?

_____

... and why?

_____
_____
_____
_____

Three goals I have for today:

1.
_____

2.
_____

3.
_____

Free space to write or draw

Write three things that you are thankful for today:

Thankful

One thing I can do for self-care today:

One dream I have for the future:

One thing I can do to care for my body today:

One person I can connect with today:

What went well for me today:

'There is no passion to be found playing small – in settling for a life that is less than the one you are capable of living.'
Nelson Mandela

 Check in

Today's date:

How am I feeling today?

😄 😊 😌 😐 ☹️ 😣

... and why?

Three goals I have for today:

1.

2.

3.

Free space to write or draw

Write three things that you are thankful for today:

_____ _____ _____

_____ _____ _____

_____ _____ _____

_____ _____ _____

_____ _____ _____

One thing I can do for self-care today:

_____

_____

_____

_____

_____

One dream I have for the future:

_____

_____

_____

_____

_____

One thing I can do to care for my body today:

_____

_____

_____

_____

_____

One person I can connect with today:

_____

_____

_____

_____

_____

What went well for me today:

_____

_____

_____

'Just get through today what you can.
You are doing your best!'
Sharon Witt

Check in

How am I feeling today?

_____

... and why?

_____

_____

_____

_____

Three goals I have for today:

1.

_____

2.

_____

3.

_____

Free space to write or draw

Write three things that you are thankful for today:

One thing I can do for
self-care today:

One dream I have for the
future:

One thing I can do to care
for my body today:

One person I can connect with today:

What went well for me today:

*'Attitude is the difference between
an ordeal and an adventure.'*

Bob Bitchin

 **Check in**

Today's date:
_____

How am I feeling today?

_____

... and why?

_____
_____
_____
_____

Three goals I have for today:

1.
_____

2.
_____

3.
_____

Free space to write or draw

Write three things that you are thankful for today:

Thankful

One thing I can do for self-care today:

One dream I have for the future:

One thing I can do to care for my body today:

One person I can connect with today:

What went well for me today:

'Always remember you have the strength, the patience and the passion to reach for the stars to change the world.'
Harriet Tubman

Check in

Today's date:

How am I feeling today?

... and why?

Three goals I have for today:

1.

2.

3.

Free space to write or draw

Write three things that you are thankful for today:

One thing I can do for self-care today:

One dream I have for the future:

One thing I can do to care for my body today:

One person I can connect with today:

What went well for me today:

'If it's out of your hands, it deserves freedom from your mind too.'

Ivan Nuru

 # Check in

Today's date:

How am I feeling today?

... and why?

Three goals I have for today:

1.

2.

3.

Free space to write or draw

Write three things that you are thankful for today:

Thankful

One thing I can do for self-care today:

One dream I have for the future:

One thing I can do to care for my body today:

One person I can connect with today:

What went well for me today:

'Grow through what you go through.'

Anon

 Check in

Today's date:

How am I feeling today?

... and why?

Three goals I have for today:

1.

2.

3.

Free space to write or draw

Write three things that you are thankful for today:

_____ _____ _____

_____ _____ _____

_____ _____ _____

_____ _____ _____

_____ _____ _____

One thing I can do for self-care today:

_____

_____

_____

_____

One dream I have for the future:

_____

_____

_____

One thing I can do to care for my body today:

_____

_____

_____

One person I can connect with today:

_____

_____

_____

_____

What went well for me today:

_____

_____

*'We are what we repeatedly do.
Excellence, then, is not an act,
but a habit.'*

Aristotle

Check in

Today's date:

How am I feeling today?

... and why?

Three goals I have for today:

1.

2.

3.

Free space to write or draw

Write three things that you are thankful for today:

One thing I can do for self-care today:

One dream I have for the future:

One thing I can do to care for my body today:

One person I can connect with today:

What went well for me today:

'Don't wait for your feelings to change to take the action. Take the action and your feelings will change.'
Barbara Baron

 **Check in**

How am I feeling today?

... and why?

Three goals I have for today:

1.

2.

3.

Free space to write or draw

Write three things that you are thankful for today:

Thankful

One thing I can do for self-care today:

One dream I have for the future:

One thing I can do to care for my body today:

One person I can connect with today:

What went well for me today:

'The difference between a stumbling block and a stepping stone is how high you raise your foot.'

Benny Lewis

Check in

How am I feeling today?

... and why?

Three goals I have for today:

1.

2.

3.

Free space to write or draw

Write three things that you are thankful for today:

One thing I can do for self-care today:

One dream I have for the future:

One thing I can do to care for my body today:

One person I can connect with today:

What went well for me today:

'If you want to lift yourself up, lift up someone else.'
Booker T. Washington

 **Check in**

Today's date:

How am I feeling today?

... and why?

Three goals I have for today:

1.

2.

3.

Free space to write or draw

Write three things that you are thankful for today:

One thing I can do for self-care today:

One dream I have for the future:

One thing I can do to care for my body today:

One person I can connect with today:

What went well for me today:

'Never do tomorrow what you can do today.
Procrastination is the thief of time.'
Charles Dickens

131

 Check in

Today's date:

How am I feeling today?

... and why?

Three goals I have for today:

1.

2.

3.

Free space to write or draw

Write three things that you are thankful for today:

One thing I can do for self-care today:

One dream I have for the future:

One thing I can do to care for my body today:

One person I can connect with today:

What went well for me today:

'Remember that not getting what you want is sometimes a wonderful stroke of luck.'

Dalai Lama

 **Check in**

Today's date:

How am I feeling today?

... and why?

Three goals I have for today:

1.

2.

3.

Free space to write or draw

Write three things that you are thankful for today:

One thing I can do for self-care today:

One dream I have for the future:

One thing I can do to care for my body today:

One person I can connect with today:

What went well for me today:

'The purpose of life is to discover your gift. The work of life is to develop it. The meaning of life is to give your gift away.'

David S. Viscott

 **Check in**

Today's date:

How am I feeling today?

... and why?

Three goals I have for today:

1.

2.

3.

Free space to write or draw

Write three things that you are thankful for today:

Thankful

One thing I can do for self-care today:

One dream I have for the future:

One thing I can do to care for my body today:

One person I can connect with today:

What went well for me today:

'There is no passion to be found in settling for a life that is less than the one you are capable of living'

Nelson Mandela

Check in

Today's date:

How am I feeling today?

... and why?

Three goals I have for today:

1.

2.

3.

Free space to write or draw

Write three things that you are thankful for today:

_____   _____   _____

_____   _____   _____

_____   _____   _____

_____   _____   _____

_____   _____   _____

One thing I can do for self-care today:

_____

_____

_____

One dream I have for the future:

_____

_____

_____

One thing I can do to care for my body today:

_____

_____

_____

One person I can connect with today:

_____

_____

_____

What went well for me today:

_____

_____

'She believed she could so she did.'

Anonymous

Check in

How am I feeling today?

... and why?

Three goals I have for today:

1.

2.

3.

Free space to write or draw

Write three things that you are thankful for today:

One thing I can do for self-care today:

One dream I have for the future:

One thing I can do to care for my body today:

One person I can connect with today:

What went well for me today:

'Friendship is born at that moment when one person says to another, 'What! You too? I thought I was the only one.'

C.S. Lewis

 **Check in**

Today's date:

How am I feeling today?

... and why?

Three goals I have for today:

1.

2.

3.

Free space to write or draw

Write three things that you are thankful for today:

One thing I can do for self-care today:

One dream I have for the future:

One thing I can do to care for my body today:

One person I can connect with today:

What went well for me today:

'You can make more friends in two months by being interested in other people than you can in two years by trying to get other people interested in you.
Dale Carnegie

Check in

How am I feeling today?

... and why?

Three goals I have for today:

1.

2.

3.

Free space to write or draw

Write three things that you are thankful for today:

One thing I can do for
self-care today:

One dream I have for the
future:

One thing I can do to care
for my body today:

One person I can connect with today:

What went well for me today:

'Kind words can be short and easy to speak,
but their echoes are truly endless.'

Mother Theresa

Check in

Today's date:

How am I feeling today?

... and why?

Three goals I have for today:

1.

2.

3.

Free space to write or draw

Write three things that you are thankful for today:

Thankful

One thing I can do for self-care today:

One dream I have for the future:

One thing I can do to care for my body today:

One person I can connect with today:

What went well for me today:

'I admire people who chose to shine even after all the storms they've been through.'

Anonymous

Check in

Today's date:

How am I feeling today?

... and why?

Three goals I have for today:

1.

2.

3.

Free space to write or draw

Write three things that you are thankful for today:

One thing I can do for self-care today:

One dream I have for the future:

One thing I can do to care for my body today:

One person I can connect with today:

What went well for me today:

'Trust the wait, embrace the uncertainty, enjoy the beauty of becoming, when nothing is certain, anything is possible.'

Unknown

Check in

How am I feeling today?

... and why?

Three goals I have for today:

1.

2.

3.

Free space to write or draw

Write three things that you are thankful for today:

One thing I can do for self-care today:

One dream I have for the future:

One thing I can do to care for my body today:

One person I can connect with today:

What went well for me today:

'Real generosity is doing something nice for someone who will never find out.'

Frank A. Clark

Check in

Today's date:

How am I feeling today?

... and why?

Three goals I have for today:

1.

2.

3.

Free space to write or draw

Write three things that you are thankful for today:

Thankful

One thing I can do for self-care today:

One dream I have for the future:

One thing I can do to care for my body today:

One person I can connect with today:

What went well for me today:

'You do not have to be rich to be generous.'
Anonymous

Check in

How am I feeling today?

... and why?

Three goals I have for today:

1.

2.

3.

Free space to write or draw

Write three things that you are thankful for today:

One thing I can do for
self-care today:

One dream I have for the
future:

One thing I can do to care
for my body today:

One person I can connect with today:

What went well for me today:

*'A little while alone in your room will prove
more valuable than anything else that could
ever be given to you.'*

Rumi

 **Check in**

Today's date:

How am I feeling today?

... and why?

Three goals I have for today:

1.

2.

3.

Free space to write or draw

Write three things that you are thankful for today:

Thankful

One thing I can do for self-care today:

One dream I have for the future:

One thing I can do to care for my body today:

One person I can connect with today:

What went well for me today:

'Do not wait until the conditions are perfect to begin. Beginning makes the conditions perfect.'

Alan Cohen

Check in

How am I feeling today?

... and why?

Three goals I have for today:

1.

2.

3.

Free space to write or draw

Write three things that you are thankful for today:

One thing I can do for self-care today:

One dream I have for the future:

One thing I can do to care for my body today:

One person I can connect with today:

What went well for me today:

'To plant a garden is to believe in tomorrow.'

Audrey Hepburn

Helpful Support
if you need it

13 11 14

Lifeline.org.au

1800 512 348

beyondblue.org.au

reachout.com